LITTLE BOOK OF
ETIQUETTE

Rufus Cavendish

summersdale

THE LITTLE BOOK OF ETIQUETTE

Copyright © Summersdale Publishers, 2014

Research by Abi McMahon

Illustrations © Shutterstock

Summersdale Publishers Ltd
46 West Street
Chichester
West Sussex
PO19 1RP
UK

www.summersdale.com

Printed and bound in the Czech Republic

ISBN: 978-1-84953- 652-3

Substantial discounts on bulk quantities of Summersdale books are available to corporations, professional associations and other organisations. For details contact Nicky Douglas by telephone: +44 (0) 1243 756902, fax: +44 (0) 1243 786300 or email: nicky@summersdale.com.

Contents

The How-Tos and Wherewithals of Etiquette

Etiquette is a code of behaviour that enables us to be our best and most considerate selves. It is not merely the faint sense of guilt that we didn't hold the door open for the person after us, or the uneasy awareness that one should help clear the plates at the party but all the tiny niceties that we can do to make loved ones and strangers alike feel good, and in the process ease our own way in society. You will find this book a useful guide to deporting yourself in social and professional situations with panache, from hosting parties, to writing, to formal occasions.

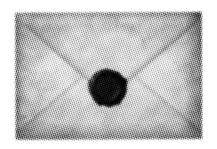

COMMUNICATION

WITH THE AGE OF TECHNOLOGY HAVING NOT ONLY DAWNED BUT PROGRESSED TO A STRONG, SUNNY NOON, WE HAVE A HOST OF TECHNIQUES TO COMMUNICATE WITH EACH OTHER.

AS LONG AS BOTH THE SENDER AND THE RECEIVER SHARE THE MEANS TO COMMUNICATE, WE MAY EXCHANGE INFORMATION IN NEAR ANY FORMAT. OF COURSE, AS NEW MEANS OF COMMUNICATION APPEAR EVER QUICKER, IT BECOMES LESS CLEAR AS TO THE ETIQUETTE; THEY LACK TRADITION, AND TRADITION IS THE BEDROCK OF ETIQUETTE. HOWEVER, AS ANY WELL-MANNERED PERSON IS AWARE, WHERE WE LACK TRADITION WE REVERT TO CONSIDERATION AND COMPASSION.

Write Letters

 A letter carries particular weight if you are writing for a special occasion such as offering congratulations or sympathy. These thoughtful notes should be handwritten; as the author has no opportunity to erase mistakes or thoughts and handwriting takes considerably longer than typing, it shows you have dedicated time and consideration to the recipient.

 Letters are also regularly used in an official capacity; often in correspondence between businesses or in applying for a job or establishing legal bonds, such as contracts. In these instances, good manners indicate that if you address the recipient by name, the appropriate sign-off is 'Yours sincerely'; if to 'Dear Sir/Madam' then your option is 'Yours faithfully'. Good sense dictates that these letters should be typed – not everyone is blessed with beautiful handwriting.

As with all methods of communication, the content should reflect the form. A page torn from a notebook, scrawled on in biro pen is a letter in name alone. A quality paper inscribed with an ink pen gives a more favourable impression. To this end, the recipient of the letter may be surprised to open a beautifully presented letter only to find it brimming with textspeak and misspellings.

The Anatomy of a Letter

First, the address, right aligned,
Second, the date, right aligned;

Third, a complimentary greeting, left aligned;

Fourth, the body of the letter, usually left aligned or centred;

Fifth, a complimentary closing, left aligned;

Sixth, your signature;

Seventh, your name, printed.

SIR, MORE THAN KISSES,
LETTERS MINGLE SOULS,
FOR THUS, FRIENDS
ABSENT SPEAK.

JOHN DONNE

Social Media

Although your thoughts are no doubt profound and your turn of phrase charming, it is worth remembering that almost everything you publish on social media is public and easily accessible. Decide with every new account you open whether it will be under your own name or a pseudonym and whom you will allow to access it. Once you have reached this decision it is your own responsibility to be aware of your audience. A misjudged post at best may alarm your grandmother, at worst offend your boss. A poor reaction at the time is not the only peril you face when updating social media – it is important to remember that even if you delete that impulsive, righteous rant on your housemate's washing-up skills, the company will retain the data. There is no opportunity for a mistake to fade with time in this age of 'memory'.

In Person

Remote communication is not the only form of communication available to us. It may be that on occasion you meet face-to-face with acquaintances and friends. It is not unreasonable to document the momentous occasion by snapping a selfie or tweeting. You could consider the possibility of initiating a sort of 'device ban' – all participants agreeing not to touch their devices or communicate on social media while you spend the time together. If this seems a touch too totalitarian for your liking then it is your responsibility to gauge the appropriateness of your actions and the reaction of your companion. Perhaps it is the chief delight of both of you to augment your time with social media, perhaps you are the recipient of frosty glares each time you reach into your pocket. Be attentive and thoughtful – this is, after all, the first principle of good etiquette.

Write an Email

 Know your audience. Emails are versatile; if using them in a formal situation apply the principles of letter writing to them. If they are intended for friends and family, by all means sign off with a picture of a cat, as is your right.

 CC (carbon copy) with caution. For an object that is intangible and immaterial, inbox space is one of the most jealously guarded things on the planet. If you cc people into emails they feel they have no interest in, you are liable to arouse ire. At work cc'ing people can be its own act of aggression – cc'ing bosses into conversations they were not previously involved in can act as a passive-aggressive threat.

 The caps lock button is not your friend. Of course you only seek to create emphasis in an otherwise emotionally cold form of communication but you come across as aggressive. If in doubt, read the email aloud, emphasising as you have in the text, realise you sound like a ninny with your **SHOUTY** capitals and remove all unnecessary formatting. Even the bold, italics or underline functions can be used unwisely.

 Press send in haste, repent at leisure, as that ancient saying goes. When writing an email you may feel a somewhat false confidence. Consider – if you would not say it to someone's face, do not send it in an email. The 'save to drafts' function was almost certainly created to halt your temper tantrums and save face. Email offers you the gift of time; use that time to cool your temper before replying to the email that provoked you.

With our ability to be in constant contact, we may easily follow the path of least resistance, offering a text or one-line message even in the most extraordinary of circumstances, and congratulate ourselves for a job well done. It behoves us to recall that we do not do things merely for our own pleasure, but to make others happy as well. By definition, the word 'special' is applied to things other or better than the ordinary. Special occasions require special attention. You do not need to pen a five-page letter every time your mother purchases a new sofa set but a happy occasion can be yet improved by a congratulatory phone call or card, as can sad feelings be soothed by a kindly worded note.

CONDOLENCE LETTERS

A letter of condolence is written in the event of bereavement and should be handwritten. An email or typed letter appears inconsiderate, or chilly. It should be brief without being curt – an overlong letter is taxing on the recipient. Nor is it the time to showcase your eloquence; restrain yourself from poetry or quotes. Enclose a genuine expression of sympathy, acknowledge the deceased by name and share an anecdote if you knew the deceased personally. If you are close to the bereaved, offering your assistance if they may need it is thoughtful. Sign off with sympathy and love.

Days of Yore

As new forms of communication spring up around us with great alacrity, others fade into their autumn years, some withering altogether. Many bemoan the abandonment of the art of letter writing in favour of emoticon-filled texts, all the while ignoring their dusty piles of fine paper and nibbed pens. However there are some traditions that we are eager to forget.

Calling cards were part of the elaborate aristocratic society rituals of getting to know connections and visiting friends. No matter how engrossing a chit-chat you may have shared over the cotillion punch, you would not expect to be received in a person's home until you had exchanged calling cards. These are mostly plain squares of card with your name and title on. A person must first visit their potential friend's house, leaving their card with a servant. If the visit and the friendship are welcome, a card would be returned. Thereon the two peoples are free to visit each other as often as they liked, as long as how often as they liked was within the hours and strictures demanded by society. Not quite as easy as a Facebook friend request after a night out!

If you wanted to give your calling card the personal touch, you would deliver it yourself, and ensure that the right hand upper corner was turned down, so no one could miss your generous gesture. You might also soothe troubled spirits by turning down the left hand lower corner, or announce your departure for a long holiday by turning down the right hand lower corner. It is to be imagined that as plain white cards were so valued for their elegance, actually writing a message would painfully mar the design.

How to

Make Your Own Paper

DIFFICULTY: ❢ ❢ ❢

REQUIRED: SCRAP PAPER SUCH AS OLD
NEWSPAPERS, MAGAZINES,
PRINTER PAPER OR NAPKINS,
A PHOTO FRAME, A SCREEN,
BLENDER, FLOWER PETALS
(OPTIONAL), LIQUID STARCH

1 Tear up the paper into small pieces.

2 Put the torn paper into a blender and fill the blender two thirds full of water.

3 Blend the paper in pulses until the mixture is a smooth pulp. Add two teaspoons of liquid starch.

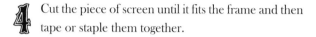

4 Cut the piece of screen until it fits the frame and then tape or staple them together.

5 Place the mould in a baking sheet and pour the pulp onto the screen. Sprinkle the petals onto the mixture if using them. Lightly shake the mixture until evenly spread.

6 Move the mould to a new, clean baking sheet and let the mixture dry.

7 Once completely dry, gently peel the paper off the mould.

8 Pen a hilarious yet heart-wrenching account of your day to friends, near or far.

TELEPHONE, N.: AN INVENTION OF THE DEVIL WHICH ABROGATES SOME OF THE ADVANTAGES OF MAKING A DISAGREEABLE PERSON KEEP HIS DISTANCE.

AMBROSE BIERCE

Telephone Etiquette

Human communication is at its strongest when face to face and we may employ all the powers at our disposal; reading body language, interpreting tone of voice, listening to the words used. Modes such as email or a telephone cut us off from helpful body language hints such as a person slowly edging away as we cheerfully prattle on, meaning it can be all too easy for misunderstandings and upsets to arise.

If you are one of the people for whom a hundred years of telecommunication has not eased the fear of making a phone call, practice is your answer. Rehearse your greeting and jot down notes on what you wish to discuss – this is especially useful if you are attempting to conduct business in some way.

You do not have the means to alleviate conversational missteps with a smile. Instead make an effort to avoid them; allow your partner time to talk, waiting if they stumble and ensure you do not interrupt.

THANK YOU CARDS

If you are ever in a position to wonder whether you should send a thank you card then it is almost certain that a thank you card should be sent. Better for friends and relatives to think you moderately over-grateful than cold hearted. As with any situation, there are no hard and fast etiquette rules for when a note must be sent but people might think you very shabby if they did not receive thanks for presents given at Christmas, birthdays, weddings, christenings and anniversaries.

If your question regarding thank you notes is when, then the answer is as soon as possible. Some recommend acting within 48 hours, others not outside of a month. There is a special understanding for newlyweds; although it is expected that they will thank loved ones for their wedding presents eventually, they should not have to cancel the honeymoon in order to do so.

DAYS OUT

A DAY SPENT IN PURSUIT OF
PLEASURE AWAY FROM THE
HOMESTEAD CAN BE A RARELY
SAVOURED TREAT BUT BRINGS
WITH IT ONE OF THE GREATEST
CHALLENGES TO POLITE
BEHAVIOUR; CONTACT WITH THE
GENERAL PUBLIC.

CONGENIAL CROWDS AND A FIZZY
ATMOSPHERE CAN GREATLY CONTRIBUTE
TO OUR ENJOYMENT OF AN EVENT, AS WE
REVEL IN THE SHARED EXPERIENCE; AND
YET BUT ONE BRUSH OF THE SHOULDER OR
UNWARRANTEDLY CHILLY GLANCE AND
WE FEEL AS IF A COLD SHROUD HAS BEEN
LAIN UPON OUR DAY. WITH A MODICUM OF
PATIENCE AND SOME EDUCATION ON GOOD
MANNERS, WE CAN ENDEAVOUR TO AT LEAST
TOLERATE OUR FELLOW MAN.

Deport Yourself in Public

 It is important to remember you are the lead player only in your own play, and but a bit part in mostly everyone else's. It pleases us to imagine that the person in front of us is walking slowly purely to thwart our trip but truth be told we have not even entered their mind. Calm yourself and remember that others' actions are at worst thoughtless, not malicious.

 Open doors for others. Do not trouble yourself on the other person's gender – your only concern should be executing a little kindness to brighten a stranger's day. Use the common sense given to you on this one – holding a door for someone who is too far to easily slip through behind you can cause sudden alarm and an awkward half-run.

 In the event of you attempting to enter somewhere as a stranger attempts to exit, the person exiting may claim right of way. This is simple scientific theory – an area can only hold a finite number of bodies, people must leave for others to enter.

Is there really a good reason you should not give way to any person you meet in your path? Do you really gain anything from engaging in a low-risk game of chicken with your fellow pedestrians, other than a foul mood? Are you so great a personage, your perambulation so vital, that you cannot take the fraction of a millisecond to step out of a fellow human's way? The answer to these questions, of course, is no.

With regards to the above point, you may be unaware that you are engaged in a slow-moving collision course as you are too engrossed in your phone. This is hardly an improvement. If you must engage in telecommunication whilst walking, pull over to the side of the pavement and endeavour to hinder as few people as possible.

THERE ARE NO STRANGERS
HERE; ONLY FRIENDS YOU
HAVEN'T YET MET.

WILLIAM BUTLER YEATS

How to

Theatre, Cinema and Dance

We posit the question; have several hundred people knowingly paid a fee to hear you talk? Unless you are featured in the show, your companion can most likely bear to wait until the interval or end of the performance to hear your thoughts. In the same vein, if you must rustle around for the largest chocolate, a moment of high action on stage is much preferable to an instance of quiet contemplation.

Discreet though you undoubtedly are, it is not enough to switch your phone to silent during the performance. In the atmospheric dark of the theatre the screen light is near-blinding for your fellow audience members and they would no doubt prefer to see the stage or screen, even if your text messages are engrossing to you. Switch your phone off.

Public Transportation

The impact you should have on your fellow traveller, if any, should be positive. You have the right to occupy the space you are in and be comfortable with it, but only as much right as every other person in the vehicle. Neither do they have more right to comfort than you – a happy compromise is its own victory. You may have to turn the volume down on your headphones so that others may not hear the mechanical churn of the bass line, they may have to draw their elbows and knees in as to not encroach on your personal space.

GREETINGS

Navigating the initial greeting when you first meet someone can hold a peculiar terror. Rest assured that everyone has got it wrong at least once and offered a cheek when a hand was extended, or presented their hand and been caught in an unexpected hug. Your first recourse should be a handshake – even if it is not the other person's first choice of greeting, they are unlikely to be offended. A hug is only appropriate for friends, but an air kiss to the cheek may be used for strangers.

Days of Yore

There have passed into obscurity many dos and don'ts of walking along the street that society once hinged upon but which may seem trivial to us in the modern age. Sartorially-minded gentlemen will be relieved they no longer have to walk between their gentlewomen friends and the road in order to protect them from carriage splashes. Ladies who relish a spot of tobacco should rest easy in the knowledge it will no longer be a fatal faux pas to enjoy a cigarette in public. And of course all may enjoy the removal of strictures that say only those of a higher position in society may greet those of lower positions; never the other way round, even if the two of you have been introduced before.

EATING WELL GIVES A SPECTACULAR JOY TO LIFE AND CONTRIBUTES IMMENSELY TO GOODWILL AND HAPPY COMPANIONSHIP.

ELSA SCHIAPARELLI

How to

Restaurant Etiquette

Of course you are not the unsavoury type to go to a restaurant and imagine that because you are ordering and another human being is fulfilling that order, that human being is in any way lesser than you. You are absolutely not the kind of person to seize on a small amount of power and use it to make your waiter feel little or humbled. Those sorts are always unbearable in restaurants and eventually find themselves devoid of invitations.

There are a number of items that should reside on the restaurant table and a number of items that have no place amongst the cutlery. Among the latter are wallets, bags, purses, phones, napkins and elbows. If you are getting up from the table during the meal, place your napkin on your chair seat. However at the end of the meal the napkin should be neatly placed to the left of your plate.

SPLITTING THE BILL

If money is not the root of all evil it is at least the root of most awkward conversations and festering grudges. As much as we try to forget that five years ago an otherwise noble friend left an unsatisfactory contribution to the tip, the knowledge wriggles interminably under the relationship. The solution is simple; discuss your payment method beforehand. The conversation does not have to be long, and would risk being boring if it were so, but a simple 'card or cash?' and 'splitting the bill or paying for individual meals?' will save you bamboozled flapping and desperate maths at the end of a pleasant meal.

Tipping practices are different across the world. Traditionally in the UK the standard tip is 10 per cent, to be shared between the party. Some restaurants specify on the receipt if the tip is included in the bill; in these cases it is usually 12.5 per cent. Insisting on using your own country's tipping practices when you are abroad and the service culture differs wildly can give you an unsavoury reputation.

CLOTHES AND ACCOUTREMENTS

OUR CLOTHES ARE OFTEN USED
AS A CERTAIN METHOD OF
MESSAGING THE PEOPLE AROUND
US, LIKE A SILENT 'HALLOA' AND
WAVE OF THE HANDKERCHIEF.

WE LIKE TO THINK THAT THEY CONVEY
PERSONALITY AND INDIVIDUALITY; THEY CAN
CERTAINLY OFTEN INDICATE OUR INTERESTS
AND THE MANNER IN WHICH WE WOULD
LIKE TO BE THOUGHT OF. TO THIS END, A
DRESS CODE MAY CHAFE AT SOME AND
BE SEEN AS A MASKING OF PERSONALITY.
HOWEVER, DRESS CODES CARRY THEIR OWN
FUNCTIONAL AND SIGNALLING PURPOSES
AND WE CAN MARK OURSELVES AS OTHER
OR UNKNOWN IF WE DO NOT FOLLOW THEM.

Daily Dress

If you were reading this guide a hundred years ago you would be informed of which suit to wear in the morning, which in the evening, the proper fabric for the countryside, the correct hat for sojourning in the city, how many times a day you must change your dress and which gloves match which sort of meal. Society's strictures are rather more relaxed now; if you wish to follow the rules alluded to above you may, of course, but you will not be shunned from polite company if you do not. Indeed the only real suspicion in modern times appears to be directed at those who wear outerwear indoors. A light fashionable scarf is acceptable but you would be best served by removing your hat, sunglasses or gloves once you have settled inside.

CLOTHING AND MANNERS DO NOT MAKE THE MAN; BUT, WHEN HE IS MADE, THEY GREATLY IMPROVE HIS APPEARANCE.

HENRY WARD BEECHER

The Workplace

Your place of work may realistically request you to follow a dress code and have a number of reasons. If your job requires you to wear protective gear, it should be possible to assume you are aware of the advantages of doing so. There is an excellent chance you are not superhuman. In the instance you work somewhere that requires a uniform, by accepting the job you have agreed to wear it.

There lies both more freedom and more danger when the dress code tends towards a set of guidelines in the place of a work-issued uniform. It may be generally understood, unless explicitly stated, that your clothes should be clean and neat. Business formal indicates a suit or smart shirt and formal trousers or skirt, with discreet, if any, accessories. Smart casual runs a rather wilder gamut but generally precludes showing the midriff, spaghetti straps, offensive or provocative images, extremely short hemlines and low necklines or translucent material on T-shirts or sandals.

DRESS
DICTIONARY

☞ *Formal or white tie*

Men, if you have been instructed to wear formal or white tie attire you should ask your tailor to make up a coat with tails, a white waistcoat, shirt and bow tie and black shoes. Alternatively, renting the same from an everyday suit store will suffice. Women should wear ballgowns. It can be a challenge to differentiate between a ballgown and an evening gown; a ballgown tends towards that air of drama.

☞ *Semi-formal or black tie*

When the invitation indicates black tie, men should wear a black dinner jacket, matching trousers, a white shirt and black bow tie. Women should wear an evening gown, traditionally floor-length.

☞ *Informal or cocktail*

The word 'informal' is meant only in the traditional sense. In this instance a T-shirt and jeans would be a grave misstep. Men should wear suits, but are not required to wear ties. For women it indicates a cocktail dress – a smart dress usually calf- or knee-length.

☞ *Smart casual*

One of the most loosely defined of the dress codes; if an invitation indicates smart casual then we usually have the opportunity to dress more in line with personal style. Smart casual is more of a collection of don'ts than dos – it does not encompass T-shirts, trainers, denim (unless very smart) or beachwear.

Dress For a Wedding

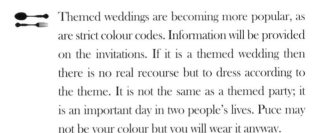 Themed weddings are becoming more popular, as are strict colour codes. Information will be provided on the invitations. If it is a themed wedding then there is no real recourse but to dress according to the theme. It is not the same as a themed party; it is an important day in two people's lives. Puce may not be your colour but you will wear it anyway.

Do not wear a white dress. Or, if you are aware that the bride's dress will be a less traditional colour, do not wear an outfit to match that colour either.

Unless otherwise stated, if the wedding ceremony takes place before 6 p.m. the suit you select should be a morning or formal suit. If after 6 p.m. then you should wear a tuxedo or tails. A wedding is not an opportunity for a comedy tie, even if humour is your shield.

Headgear is no longer as mandatory as it once was but if you have the opportunity to wear an over-sized and unusual hat, there is no reason not to take it. Alternatively, ladies and very adventurous men, you may prefer a fascinator.

It seems there will never be an easy time to be a courting couple; there will always be art and column space dedicated to the challenge of communicating your best intentions to your beloved. However rocky the modern path to love may be, present-day lovers may at least rest easy that they do not have to interpret the language of hand fans. In the eighteeth and nineteenth century hand fans were popular ladies' accessories and by the 1800s guidebooks were being published on the 'language of fans'. Although it is uncertain to what extent these books were tongue-in-cheek, they purported to help ardent swains in interpreting the secret messages their sweethearts were sending by holding their fans just so. A fan tilted to obscure the mouth, nose and left eye apparently meant 'I am engaged', although one might hope that would crop up in conversation before the courtship started. More hopefully for lovesick men, a half-open fan covering the mouth and nose broadcast 'I love you'. It is to be hoped that such signals would only reach their intended and no startled bystanders were to be surprised by a lady they had never met confessing their love.

Tie a Bow Tie

1 The end on the right should hang slightly lower than the end on the left, with around an inch and a half's difference.

2 Cross the right end over the left and thread through the loop.

3 Double up the shorter end and put it across the collar points. This will form the front loop.

4 Pinch the loop with your right hand and drop the other end over the front.

5 Pass the hanging end up behind the front loop.

6 Thread the loop that this creates through the knot behind the front loop, ensuring the ends are even length. Tighten to secure.

7 Strut confidently through town, certain in the knowledge you look officially natty.

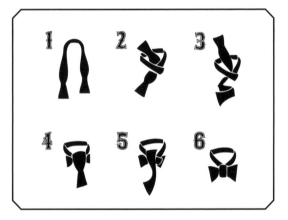

THROUGH TATTERED CLOTHES SMALL VICES DO APPEAR; ROBES AND FUR'D GOWNS HIDE THEM ALL.

WILLIAM SHAKESPEARE

Sporting Clubs and Other

For a majority of sporting clubs merely ensuring your spandex appears unstained and not too pungent is satisfactory; you will not be barred from entry at the gym if you leave your tie at home. However there are some sporting arenas that would not look so kindly upon your sartorial laxity. Of course there are conventions – one might automatically avoid wearing a rugby shirt to football practice – but for some these conventions are tempered with time to a tradition.

For this reason it is always best to check the dress code when you join any new club, be it sporting or social. Although somewhat relaxed in recent years, one of the most infamously stringent rule-setters are golfing clubs. If you were to attempt to play in trainers a collective shiver would go down the spines of members, similarly combats or denim jeans would have a chilly reception. Instead members are expected to wear golf shoes, tailored trousers or shorts are a must and your shirt must have a collar. There is no word on what to expect if your hat is worn peak-backwards instead of peak-forwards but it will likely not be kind.

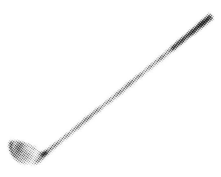

ASCOT

No doubt Ascot is a fixture in your yearly calendar and you simply cannot resist a small flutter on the royal horse. For those rare persons who are not regular attendees, dressing for Ascot is something to be carefully considered. There are so few areas of modern life where dress code is really enforced that attending an event where it is positively relished can be daunting.

Ladies, skirts should fall on or below the knee. Strapless and spaghetti strap dresses should be an anathema to you and regardless of how well that sheer lace illusion dress suits you, anything of that ilk should be left at home. Ascot regulations state that a hat, fascinator or headpiece should be worn at all times.

Gentlemen, unlike ladies your dress code relaxes significantly between the Royal Enclosure and Grandstand Admission. For the latter a suit with shirt, tie and black shoes will be your passport to refinement, for the former a black or grey morning suit replete with top hat. Ascot regulations specify that customisation of top hats is not permitted.

SOCIAL
OCCASIONS

THE ONLY RULE A SOCIAL
OCCASION MUST REALLY
ADHERE TO IS THAT IT SHOULD
BE DESIGNED AS A GOOD TIME
TO BE ENJOYED BY ALL.

IF FUN IS HAD THEN YOU MAY ENJOY YOURSELF IN WHICHEVER WAY YOUR FANCY TAKES YOU. IT MAY BE A HANDFUL OF YOUR CLOSEST FRIENDS OR AN OPEN INVITATION TO EVERY PERSON YOU HAVE EVER SPOKEN TO, OR A CELEBRATION OF YOUR BIRTHDAY OR SIMPLY THE FACT IT IS THE THIRD SATURDAY OF THE MONTH, IF THE SOCIAL NICETIES ARE OBSERVED YOUR PARTY MAY BE REASONABLY DEPENDED ON TO BE A JOLLY TIME.

For Hosts

 Communicate with your guests. Timely invitations are of great importance, along with providing general information about date, time, location, potential theme and whether or not to bring anything. If you are celebrating an immovable feast or national holiday it is important to issue invitations even earlier than usual, as people's time is likely to be swiftly booked.

 Be aware of the demands you are making on your guests. It may be that your Day of the Dead-themed Halloween party is the very realisation of all your dreams but if your closest friends have a peculiar horror of face paint and piñatas it is unlikely your celebration will be well-attended. As the principle purpose of a party is for all to enjoy themselves, it would be unbecoming to have a fit of pique over the matter. Nobody should be required to attend your party at the expense of their own enjoyment.

A host is not merely the person at whose house the party is taking place, or the subject of the celebration. A good host must act as the oil lubricating the wheels of the party: introducing strangers, facilitating conversation when there are lulls, ensuring their guests' needs are met and their glasses full.

 Reserve a room for your guests' possessions, such as coats and bags. If the party is taking place at your residence you assume responsibility for not only your guests but any sundries they may bring. It is far easier to allocate a space for everything to be kept in than to spend the small hours of your party searching your home for a missing bag and three near-identical black jackets.

 If you expect young guests to be attending, there should be at least one child-friendly area with entertainment. Your adult guests may be sufficiently entertained by your scintillating conversation, but young minds require rather more stimulation.

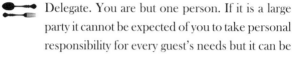 Delegate. You are but one person. If it is a large party it cannot be expected of you to take personal responsibility for every guest's needs but it can be expected that those needs should be taken care of. Appointing a trusty second will also ease the pressure from you; a host having histrionics in the bathroom is of no use to anyone.

This guide hesitates to mention such things but as the subject of bathrooms has arisen – have twice as much toilet roll as you expect to use and keep the replacements in plain sight. Of course, you don't need an explanation as to why.

LET US CELEBRATE THE OCCASION WITH WINE AND SWEET WORDS.

PLAUTUS

The Work Party

As the Christmas season rolls merrily around there appears to be an iron-clad rule that bears repeating: do not get too drunk at your work party. There is not a single situation that can be conceived of where it would be a good idea to get too drunk at your work party. It matters not a fig if the music is bad, the company is not your first choice in companions or the food was provided sparingly at best. Professionalism is being your best and most considered self – even your sober self must think twice when talking to your colleagues; your drunk self has too many opportunities to offend and scandalise.

The Garden Party

Hosts, put your faith in your own planning rather than the weather. If your intention is to hold your festivity outside, especially in the evening, be prepared to erect some form of shelter, such as a marquee, in the event that the weather is not complicit in your plans. Provide seating, encroaching on the kindness of friends or family if you do not have sufficient garden furniture yourself. Even if you are hosting a picnic, provide some chairs in addition to blankets. Unless your friends solely comprise of the young and very fit, back support will be welcome to many.

Guests, perhaps this is not the party to debut your new spike heels. It is extremely unlikely your host's lawn is in desperate need of repeated puncturing.

For Guests

 A swift and definite answer is the most helpful. Although your host may almost certainly be bereft if you are not able to attend, it is likely they will recover tolerably well and fill your space with another guest. Requesting to bring a plus-one is more acceptable in the case of a large party.

 Respect the spoken and unspoken boundaries. If your host asks you to not enter a certain area, then that area is out of bounds. A shut door also indicates 'do not enter'. Closed cupboards are not yours to rifle through. If you have a request or an idea takes your fancy, your host should be your first point of call. If the party is taking place at a venue then you will not know what arrangement your host has with the proprietors. If it is at their home your host has a reasonable expectation of privacy where they have requested it.

Overindulgence may feel good, but often leaves a sad impression on your hosts and fellow guests. Imbibing more than you should may be acceptable amongst your close group of friends but it is wise to be wary if you aren't acquainted with the majority of the party. Equally, delicious though the fare may be, if there are buffet-style provisions take care to only eat your fair share.

 Be a willing participant. It will be a drag on everyone's moods if you sulk around parlour games. Conversely don't get so involved in the spirit of the competition that you come across a bad loser (or bad winner). You are not a tipsy Olympian.

 The most thoughtful guest asks if they can bring anything and a token gift for the host is always welcome. If you stay to the end of the party, assist in cleaning up. You have had an enjoyable time, cleaning up is a small way to thank the person who facilitated that.

THE GIFT OF WINE AND SONG

There is a distinct line between bringing a gift for the host and a gift for the party. If you have brought a gift for the host then it is for the host alone – they decide what is to be done with it and you may have no expectations to share it. If you have brought something to the party, such as alcohol or food, by all means avail yourself of it while you are there. But whatever you bring remains behind – even if you have spent five hours crafting the finest pavlova known to man and there has been but one slice taken from it, you must leave it behind. A good night and empty bottles are not the host's only reward.

Society has always endeavoured to find something to be scandalised by and dancing has been a favourite of gossip-mongers and moralisers for centuries. Even in the modern day column inches are filled with gasping outrage at gyrating young people, although times have perhaps moved on slightly from the fourth century when the Christian church condemned dancing as the devil's work. One of the biggest scandals to rock society was in the nineteenth century, when the royal court danced the waltz.

Now a bedazzled and befeathered staple of television dancing shows, the waltz was considered a shocking show of salaciousness, with newspapers of the time going as far as to call it a 'prostitutes" dance. The couples dancing this public display of fornication would have to stand so close as to almost (if one considers a foot of space almost) be touching and the gentleman's hand would rest upon the lady's shoulder as they moved. Moral advice of the day was for parents not to allow their daughters to dance, lest they be led down a dark path. It all makes Aunty Jilly's dancing at family soirées sound positively angelic.

Make Bunting

DIFFICULTY: 🍴 🍴 🍴 🍴

REQUIRED: FELT. CARDBOARD. NEEDLE. THREAD. BIAS BINDING TAPE. PINKING SHEARS

1   Cut a triangle template from cardboard and pin it to the felt

2   Using pinking shears to avoid fraying, cut out the triangle. Repeat until you are satisfied you have enough to create your bunting.

3   Sew the triangles to the binding tape using a running stitch, ensuring they are evenly spaced along the tape.

4   Strew the bunting about the house.

TRUE HAPPINESS ARISES, IN THE FIRST PLACE, FROM THE ENJOYMENT OF ONE'S SELF, AND IN THE NEXT, FROM THE FRIENDSHIP AND CONVERSATION OF A FEW SELECT COMPANIONS.

JOSEPH ADDISON

THE DINNER PARTY

A DINNER PARTY – WHAT COULD
BE MORE PLEASANT THAN AN
EVENING OF CONVERSATION,
FINE FOOD AND LIBATION?

WHILE WE MAY NO LONGER WAKE IN A
COLD SWEAT, IMAGINING WE ACCIDENTALLY
OMITTED THE WHITE SOUP OR THAT THE
SERVANTS BROKE RANKS AND ATTEMPTED
CHIT-CHAT, HOSTING OR ATTENDING A DINNER
PARTY REMAINS ONE OF THE MORE FORMAL
EVENTS IN ONE'S CALENDAR. FEAR NOT,
THESE PITFALLS ARE EASILY NAVIGATED
WITH GOOD MANNERS AND THE AID OF A
TRUSTWORTHY GUIDE TO ETIQUETTE.

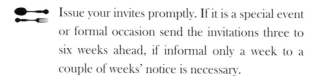

How to

For Hosts

- Issue your invites promptly. If it is a special event or formal occasion send the invitations three to six weeks ahead, if informal only a week to a couple of weeks' notice is necessary.

- Communication is key. Your guests should be aware of any theme or dress code in addition to the RSVP deadline. It is your responsibility to inquire as to any dietary requirements or allergies your guests may have.

- Now is not the time for daring adventure. If you must recreate the seven-stage fusion main you enjoyed at that restaurant one time, at least practise it once in its entirety prior to the evening.

- Be firm, yet flexible. You are a reed in the wind. Have a portion of your meal prepared ahead of time, have drinks and refreshments on hand

and work to a timesheet, but do not succumb to hysterics if your pastry is not perfectly golden. Your guests are inclined to have a good time regardless.

For Guests

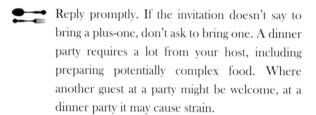 Reply promptly. If the invitation doesn't say to bring a plus-one, don't ask to bring one. A dinner party requires a lot from your host, including preparing potentially complex food. Where another guest at a party might be welcome, at a dinner party it may cause strain.

Arrive even more promptly. Unless your host is very confident, they have more than likely started the preparations before you were scheduled to arrive and your lateness will throw a spanner of unwieldy proportions into the mix.

Ask your host what you can do or bring to help. Holding a dinner party often requires a decent portion of a person's monetary and time resources. Offering to take responsibility for the wine or sweet can go a long way to help. Some hosts may be grateful for the assistance, especially if they are hosting a large group. However, you will merely clutter the kitchen if you press your suit after your offer of help is refused.

 Bring a gift. Regardless of whether your host has requested you bring anything, something to drink or a small offering such as flowers will be readily accepted. They are a token of your thanks in advance and can often ease the process for a harassed host.

 Help clear the table between courses. You are visiting your friend, not a restaurant.

 Say 'thank you'. The more flamboyantly minded of you may prefer to send a pleasing note or card but a text or message on social media can do as well. This should be sent within a couple of days of having attended the event.

AT A DINNER PARTY ONE
SHOULD EAT WISELY BUT
NOT TOO WELL, AND TALK
WELL BUT NOT TOO WISELY.

W. SOMERSET MAUGHAM

Phones and Electronic Devices

A successful dinner party's primary characteristic is quality: quality food, quality company, quality time. A uniquely modern challenge to this happy arrangement is technology. The party can often be disrupted or distracted by people updating their social media, texting or taking excessive amounts of photos. One solution is for the host to request a 'phone stack' where everyone, including the host, places their phones face down in the centre of the table. The first to reach for their device receives a forfeit; this can range in strength of suffering from assuming responsibility for the washing up, eating something unpleasant or a more physical challenge, perhaps ten hearty press-ups.

Music

Hosts, your music should be subdued and a friend to conversation. Avoid anything aurally challenging – now is not the time to unveil your latest album of Tuvan throat singing. Fear not, your guests are already aware your music taste is nonpareil, otherwise they would not consent to dine with you.

Guests, you are all acquainted with that jolly gentleman or lady who appears to attend friends' events purely to criticise the music and spend the evening surgically attached to the player. Under no circumstances should you be that individual.

Quick and Easy

When hosting, remember that your primary objective is for you and your guests to enjoy yourselves. If you would like to have a group of friends round to make merry over victuals but are perhaps not an infamously good cook or you don't have infinite time to prepare a meal, there are other options available to you. Perhaps you would like to host a 'potluck dinner' where you provide the essentials and the guests bring a dish each, or even just have everyone round for a fancy takeaway. The only condition to enjoyment is that you observe the niceties of hosting and invite company you take pleasure in.

RSVP

Not merely a collection of unconnected letters indicating that you are required to reply, RSVP stands for *répondez s'il vous plaît*, French for 'please reply'. The method of invitation will usually indicate the manner in which you are expected to reply. A physical invitation such as a card may contain a section to mark and return, an invite on social media may have a button you can press to provide your attendance status. Regardless of the manner in which you reply, a prompt reply is the first in polite behaviour. Your host cannot start to plan their meal and other arrangements if you insist on wavering with the milquetoast 'maybe'.

Lay the Table

 There has been much made of the nature of etiquette within these pages, and this book squarely places the emphasis on etiquette as niceties rather than necessities. However, though we celebrate the fact that we will not be cut from all society if a fork is out of place, this does not mean that should you wish to hold an elaborate dinner party, you should have the means.

 There is a certain pleasantness in the ritual of a fine dinner, the to-ing and fro-ing of courses, the opportunity to sit at length with friends and sample every sort of nourishment the earth has to offer. There are also certain pitfalls; one must have a large amount of cutlery and tableware else one is frantically washing up between courses. One must also be aware of the order of things.

The first step is to lay your table correctly. You may add or remove courses as you wish; simply add or remove the corresponding cutlery and glassware, preserving the order in which things are laid. The glasses should come to the table with the course they accompany.

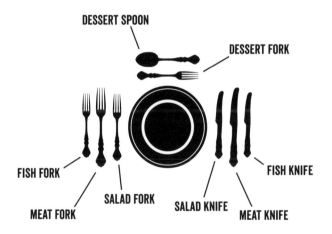

DESSERT SPOON

DESSERT FORK

FISH FORK

MEAT FORK

SALAD FORK

SALAD KNIFE

MEAT KNIFE

FISH KNIFE

Order of Wine

Unless your schedule is particularly punishing or your guests all coincidentally delayed, allow an hour at the beginning of your party for guests to mingle. Serve up a sparkling wine or light cocktail to lubricate conversation – you want your guests in a good mood but still able to work their way around a soup spoon. If you have particular concerns about fare you'll be serving, maybe two glasses will help them a little on their way!

It is up to you whether you would prefer to serve one bottle of wine throughout the meal or match your refreshments to the course you are serving. If opting for the former, calculate the number of bottles required to fully satisfy your guests and not appear stingy. Unless your guests are particularly voracious then about three glasses, or a bottle per person, should quench their dinnertime thirst. If you prefer the latter approach, here follows a guide to order of service for alcohol. Of course, wine is a thing that human beings cannot help but have opinions about – the list that follows is comprehensive but cannot be relied upon to satisfy tipsy commentators.

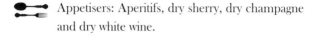

Appetisers: Aperitifs, dry sherry, dry champagne and dry white wine.

Soup: If the soup's ingredients include a sherry it is advisable to also serve a sherry. Otherwise a white wine or dry champagne will serve.

Fish: Remain with the white wine for fish dishes, or if you would rather, dry champagne.

Fowl: Dishes featuring fowl such as chicken, turkey, duck or pigeon are also best suited by a dry white wine or dry champagne.

Game: If pheasants, grouse, quail or other game birds are on the menu, change to a dry red wine to match the dish.

Red meat: A dry red wine will match your red meat to the best effect.

Salad: If one of your courses is salad no wine is served, although do not be so daring as to attempt to remove any glasses from people's hands!

Cheese: The cheese course signals the end of the meal, starting or sometimes replacing the dessert. To treat it as such, serve with a dessert wine.

Dessert: As is rather indicated by the name, match your dessert with a dessert wine. If you have a chocolate dessert, or chocolate course, you may want to compound the indulgence with a port or cream sherry.

Liqueur: As with cheese, serving a liqueur can occasionally be served in place of the dessert course, or to finish the meal, depending on your guests' tastes.

Days of Yore

It is part of the pleasing ritual of the dinner party that one's guests should ask on invitation, 'should I bring anything', to which the host replies 'only yourself', fully expecting a defiant bottle of wine or small gift. Perambulate back a couple of hundred years and one might find a different answer, that of 'only your knife and spoon'. For many years the only really established form of cutlery at the table was the knife; by the fouteenth century forks and spoons were in play but guests were expected to bring those themselves, carrying them in a special case wherever they travelled. As with anything new, the fork was viewed at first by English society as suspicious, suffering the accusation that the cutlery was effeminate and unnecessary when humans had hands. The wealthy eventually adopted it as a symbol of fashionable society, although the stiff-upper-lipped British Navy only lifted the ban on 'effeminate' forks in the nineteenth century.

THE SOFT EXTRACTIVE
NOTE OF AN AGED CORK
BEING WITHDRAWN HAS
THE TRUE SOUND OF A MAN
OPENING HIS HEART.

WILLIAM S. BENWELL